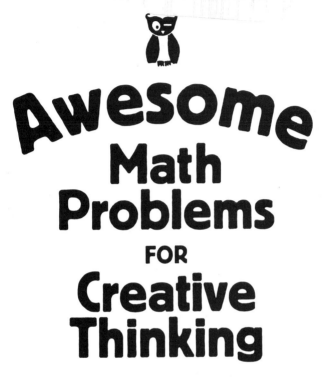

Awesome
Math
Problems
FOR
Creative
Thinking

Carole E. Greenes
Carol R. Findell
M. Katherine Gavin
Linda Jensen Sheffield

**Wright Group
McGraw-Hill**

Acknowledgments

EDITOR Harriet Slonim

PROJECT EDITOR Janet Pittock

DESIGN DIRECTOR Karen Lee Stack

DESIGN Laurie Szujewska

COVER ILLUSTRATION Bonni Evensen

ILLUSTRATION Bonni Evensen

TYPESETTING Laurie Szujewska

ISBN 0-7622-1282-9
Customer Service 800-624-0822
www.creativepublications.com
2 3 4 5 6 7 8 BAN 05 04 03 02

THIS BOOK BELONGS TO:

_____

We wrote this book just for you. It's filled with our favorite problems. Some are hard. Others are really hard. Still others are really, really hard. (These are the ones at the end of the book.)

What's great about these problems is that when you do them you get to use what you know about math in different ways. And doing them will help you learn lots more about math, too. You can work on the problems alone or work with someone who also has this book.

Take this book along with you everywhere. This way you can do the problems while you're traveling, at recess, watching TV, eating lunch, under the covers, and over e-mail. You get the picture. Just do 'em!

Have Fun!

Coin Quest!

What six coins are in this bank?

On the Way to 200

Here is the start of a two-hundred chart.

1	2	3	4	5	6	7	8	9	10
11	12	13	14	15	16	17	18	19	20
21	22	23	24	25	26	27	28	29	30
31	32	33	34						

Imagine the numbers going on and on to 200.

Fill in the numbers that belong on this part of the chart.

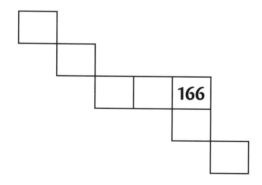

Just a Matter of Time

What time is it when the sum of the digits on a digital clock is the greatest?

A "Month" of Sundays

Christy is walking to school on September 2 and thinking about her birthday on September 30. She realizes that there will be five Sundays this month.

On what day of the week will Christy's birthday be?

Six Slices or Eight?

Wanda walked into Pepe's Pizza Place.
She ordered a whole pizza for herself.
"Do you want it cut into 6 slices or 8?" Pepe asked.
"I am not that hungry" Wanda said. "Better make it just 6!"

What is wrong with Wanda's thinking?

How Many Heads?

You can use:

4 wigs

2 noses

3 mouths

2 pairs of eyes

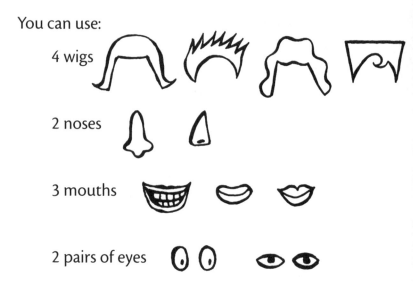

How many different sweet-potato heads can you make?

Number Cube

The faces of this cube show consecutive counting numbers.

What is the greatest number that could be on the cube?

Some Sums

The sums go in the circles.
But some sums are missing!

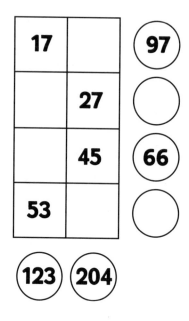

Add across.
Add down.

Write the missing addends and the missing sums.

Marble Garble

Riley bought a bag of marbles. There are twice as many red marbles as yellow marbles in the bag. The total number of marbles is a multiple of 4.

What is the fewest number of marbles that could be in the bag?

SASHA'S PATTERN

Sasha loves using her gel pen to write her name again and again.

If she keeps going, what will be the 91st letter?

SASHASASHASASHASASHA...

Three Shapes

Same shapes have same values.
Different shapes have different values.

Find the value of each shape.

$\square$ + $\square$ + 6 = 24

$\square$ + $\bigcirc$ + $\hexagon$ = 14

$\hexagon$ + $\hexagon$ + $\hexagon$ + 10 = 19

$\square$ = _____

$\bigcirc$ = _____

$\hexagon$ = _____

Apples and Oranges

Granny Smith made a great big fruit salad based on this recipe. She used 42 pieces of fruit in all.

How many apples did Granny use in her great big fruit salad?

SMALL FRUIT SALAD

Ingredients:

- ◉ 3 apples
- ◉ 4 oranges

Peel fruit.
Cut into small pieces.
Mix well.

Where is 79?

Pretend that the pattern continues.

In which row is 79?

Row 1	1	2	3	4	5
Row 2	6	7	8	9	10
Row 3	11	12	13	14	15
Row 4	16	17	18	19	20
Row 5	21	22	23	24	25

In the Middle

A book starts on page 1.
It ends on page 401.

What is the number of the page in the middle?

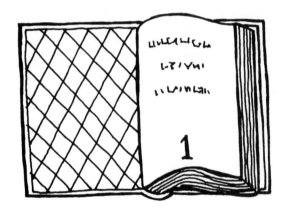

Empty Shapes

Same shapes have same values.
Different shapes have different values.
Add across. Add down.
The numbers in the circles are row and column sums.

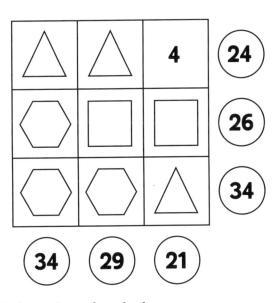

Find the value of each shape.

Same Sums

7, 8, 9, 10, 11, and 12 are on this number cube.
Pairs of numbers on opposite faces add up to a sum.
That sum is the same for all pairs of numbers on
opposite faces.

What number is on the bottom face?

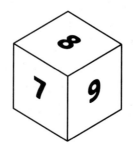

The Better Buy

Which bag of cookies is the better buy,
the Super Size or the Snack Size?

How do you know?

To find the better buy,
compare prices for
the same number of
cookies.

Think "Snow"!

Pam had a square piece of paper.
She folded it in half.
Then she folded it in half again.
She made two cuts in the folded paper.
When Pam unfolded the paper, she held up a snowflake!

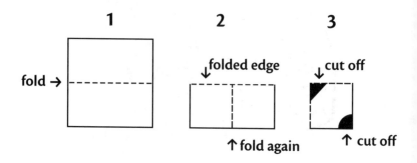

Draw Pam's snowflake here.

Shape Totals

Same shapes have same values.
Different shapes have different values.

Find the value of each shape.

$\triangle$ + $\bigcirc$ + $\bigcirc$ = **19**

$\triangle$ + $\square$ = **15**

$\triangle$ + $\bigcirc$ = **13**

$\square$ = _____

$\triangle$ = _____

$\bigcirc$ = _____

Pounds-a-Plenty

Same shapes have the same weights.
Different shapes have different weights.

Find the weight of each shape.

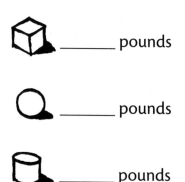

_____ pounds

_____ pounds

_____ pounds

Nine Is Fine

Write +, −, or × in each circle to complete a true number sentence.

1 ◯ 3 ◯ 8 ◯ 4 ◯ 2 = 9

 ANSWER IS ON PAGE 56

Yikes!

60 legs!
8 bugs!
Some are ants.
Some are spiders.

How many of each are there?

An ant is an insect.
It has 6 legs.
A spider is an arachnid.
It has 8 legs.

MATTHEW'S PATTERN

Sasha's brother Matthew borrowed her gel pen.

If he keeps on writing his name over and over like this, how many T's will there be in the first 140 letters?

MATTHEWMATTHEWMATTHEW...

Get a Homer!

Use the numbers on the sign.

Put one number on each line so that the story makes sense.

There are_____ bases on a baseball field.

The distance from each base to the next is_____ feet.

From the pitcher's mound to home plate is

_____ feet, _____ inches.

If you get a homer and run around all the bases just once,

you'll run_____ feet.

Now You See Them...
Now You Don't

You can see two sides and the top of this building made of cubes. Imagine you can see all of the sides.

What is the least number of cubes there can be in this building?

What is the greatest number of cubes?

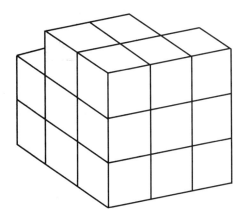

Try for "A" 13!

Write a different one-digit number in each circle so that the sum of the numbers along each line is 13.

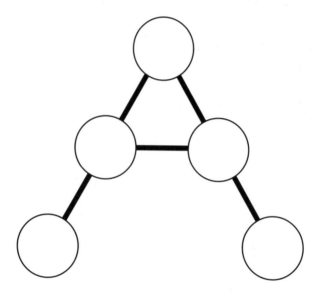

Figure Out the Figure

Each figure below has a different number of dots.
The figures form a pattern. Pretend that the pattern goes
on and on.

Which figure will have 40 dots?

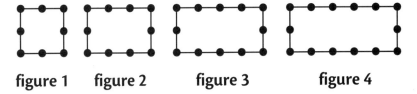

figure 1   figure 2   figure 3   figure 4

Moving Money

Three kids, Tyler, Chris, and Justine want to share their money equally. They can do this if each kid gives just one coin to one of the other kids.

Which kids exchange which coins?

Doubly Delicious

Get ready to pick two flavors of ice cream for a double sundae.

How many different two-flavor combinations could you pick?

ICE CREAM FLAVORS

CHOCOLATE
VANILLA
STRAWBERRY
ORANGE
PEACH
BANANA

A Walking Problem

Tim walked a total of 30 blocks in 5 days.
Each day he walked 3 more blocks than he had
the day before.

How many blocks did Tim walk on the first day?

Number Puzzle

Same shapes have same numbers.
Different shapes have different numbers.

If

$$\begin{array}{rcc} & \square & \triangle \\ + & \triangle & \square \\ \hline 1 & 6 & 5 \end{array}$$

then find this product.

$$2 \times (\square + \triangle) = ____$$

  ANSWER IS ON PAGE 56

Stamp It!

Peggy has 5 stamps.
Each one is worth either 33¢, 32¢, or 24¢.
The total value of her stamps is $1.46.

How many of each stamp does Peggy have?

Birthday Gift

Chris got a gift of money for his birthday.
He spent half the money on a T-shirt.
He spent half of what was left on baseball cards.
After he spent $1.00 for popcorn, he had $4.00 left.

How much money did Chris get for his birthday?

Roll 'Em

You have two number cubes, each numbered
1, 2, 3, 4, 5, 6.

Pretend you roll the cubes once and multiply the
numbers on the top faces.

**What is the probability that the product would be
an even multiple of 3?**

Multiples of 3 are
the numbers you say
when you count by 3's.
For example,
some multiples of 3
are "3, 6, and 9."

Ripped Receipt

Whoops! The receipt got ripped!

Use the clues to fill in the prices.

- ⊙ The chicken is 5¢ more than twice the cost of milk.

- ⊙ The orange juice costs 18¢ less than three times the price of the cheese.

- ⊙ The cereal costs 1 dollar, 2 dimes, and 1 penny less than 5 dollars.

SAL'S SUPERMARKET

CARROTS	$ 0.89
CHEESE	$ 0.99
POTATOES	$ 2.00
MILK	$ 1.50
CEREAL	_____
CHICKEN	_____
ORANGE JUICE	_____
TAX	$ 0.83
TOTAL	_____

The Frosting on the Cake

Laura's birthday cake is 12 inches long and 8 inches wide.
It is frosted on the top and on all four sides.
Laura cuts the cake into 2-inch squares.

How many more of the pieces have frosting on two sides than on one side?

Watch the Hands

How many times do the hands of a watch
pass each other between noon and midnight?

This one's pretty tricky!
You may want to use a
real watch or clock to
help you.

Best Friend

Dan, Dora, Doug, Diane, and Dave are the only people in the ticket line at the movies.

Use these clues to find Dan's best friend.

- ◉ The first and last people in the line are boys.

- ◉ Dave is not first or last.

- ◉ Dora is standing right between Doug and Diane.

- ◉ Dan's best friend is standing right in front of him in the line.

Who is Dan's best friend?

Folding Folly

Get a square piece of paper.
Fold one corner back so that you can't see the folded part.
Name the new shape you have left.

How many different shapes can you make with just one fold?

Who Likes Basketball?

Andrew, Betty, Kenesha, and Dan are best friends.
Two are 8 years old, one is 9, and one is 10.
They each have a favorite sport—soccer, basketball,
swimming, and baseball.

**Use these clues to find whose favorite sport is
basketball.**

- Andrew and Kenesha are twins.

- The oldest of the friends plays baseball
  every morning.

- Dan goes to the pool every morning in
  the summer.

- Kenesha is a great goalie.

One Brick at a Time

Color each brick.
Bricks that touch must be different colors.
Use the fewest number of different colors possible.

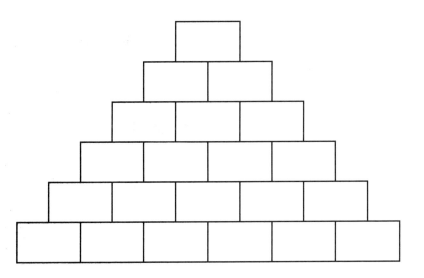

Remember, bricks that touch
can't be the same color!

How many colors did you use?

Kids and Bikes

Four families live on our street.
Their last names are Rondo, Chin, Valdez, and Clark.
The graph shows how many kids and how many bikes
each family has.

Use the clues to name the family with the fewest kids.

⊙ There are more bikes than kids in
each of the Valdez and Chin families.

⊙ There are the same number of bikes
as kids in the Rondo family.

⊙ There are two more kids in the Clark
family than in the Valdez family.

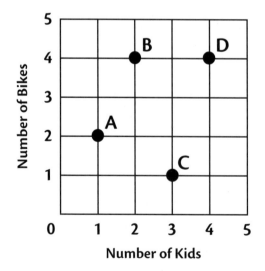

A Mystery

Latisha invited me to a mystery party.
The first mystery is to figure out her house number!

**Follow the clues on the invitation to find
Latisha's house number.**

? Come to a ?
Mystery Party?
Sunday ~ March 3

- My house number has
  four digits.

- Each digit is greater than
  the digit just to its left.

- The first digit at the left is
  an even number.

- The difference between the
  first digit and the second is 1.

- The last digit is one more
  than the third digit.

- The four digits add up to 20.

I live at _____ Elmwood Drive.

Words Worth

Use letters as numbers!
Let A = 1, B = 2, C = 3, and so on.

Find a three-letter word with a value of 56 that names a place.

_____ _____ _____ = 56

Find a four-letter word with a value of 26 that names an animal.

_____ _____ _____ _____ = 26

Real or Fake?

Mr. Gem is a jeweler. He needs to find out how much real gold is in this "gold" necklace. If the necklace is real gold, it will weigh 15 grams.

These are Mr. Gem's weights.

How can Mr. Gem use the weights to find out if the necklace weighs 15 grams?

Grid of Squares

Place the numbers 1 through 9 in the grid of squares. (Some of these numbers are already there.)

The sum of the numbers in each row goes in the circle at the right.

The sum of the numbers in each column goes in the circle below.

Fill in the squares.
Fill in the circles.

	1	5	◯
	7		12
6			23
12	17	◯	

Pizza with the Works

Kerry ordered a pizza with pepperoni, mushrooms, and olives.

When the pizza arrived, Kerry counted:

- 27 pieces of toppings.

- twice as many mushrooms as pieces of pepperoni.

- 3 fewer olives than mushrooms.

How many pieces of each kind of topping were there?

_____ pepperoni

_____ mushrooms

_____ olives

License Plate Quiz

Six digits belong on this license plate.

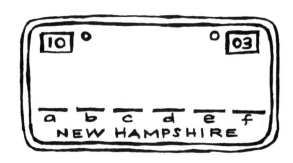

Use the clues to help you find them.

- ⦿ The digits are all different.
- ⦿ $d + e = d$
- ⦿ b, c, and f are the only odd numbers
- ⦿ $c \times b = c$
- ⦿ $c < 5$
- ⦿ $f < 7$
- ⦿ $c - a = b$
- ⦿ $d - f = c$

Full House

How many people live in each kid's house?

Use the clues to find out.
Write each kid's name below the graph.

- ◉ In Kristen's house, there are 3 times as many people as pets.

- ◉ There is an odd number of people and an odd number of pets in Ben's house.

- ◉ There is a total of 9 people and pets in Lisa's house, with more pets than people.

- ◉ In Mike's house, there are 3 fewer pets than people.

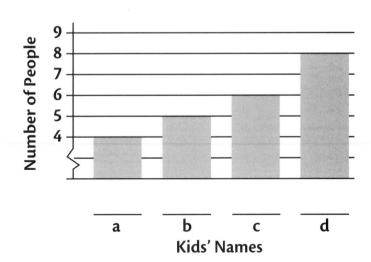

Corner Numbers

Write a different number in each circle.
The sum of the numbers in connected circles must equal
the number on the line that connects them.

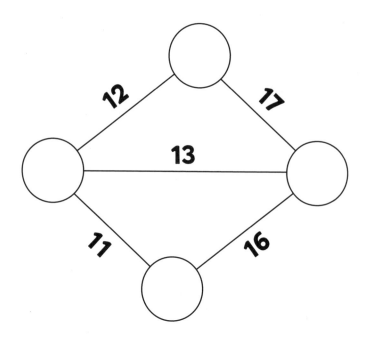

Answers ☀☀☀☀☀☀☀☀☀☀☀☀☀

Apples and Oranges

18 apples. There are 7 pieces of fruit in the small fruit salad. 42 ÷ 7 = 6 means that the great big fruit salad has 6 times the number of pieces of fruit. 6 × 3 apples = 18 apples.

Apples	Oranges	Total pieces of fruit
3	4	7
6	8	14
9	12	21
12	16	28
15	20	35
18	24	42

Best Friend

Dave. Doug is first in line. Dora is second. Diane is third. Dave is fourth. Dan is fifth.

The Better Buy

Better buy: Super Size
Super Size—9 cookies for $3.00.
$3.00 ÷ 9 is about 33¢ for 1 cookie.
Snack Size—6 cookies for $2.40.
$2.40 ÷ 6 is 40¢ for 1 cookie.
33¢ is less than 40¢
or Super Size—3 cookies for $1.00.
Snack Size—3 cookies for $1.20.
$1.00 is less than $1.20.

Birthday Gift

$20. Chris had $4.00 left. He had $5.00 before he bought popcorn. He had $10.00 before he bought the baseball cards. So he had $20.00 before he bought the T-shirt.

Coin Quest

1 half dollar, 1 quarter, 1 nickel, 3 pennies

Corner Numbers

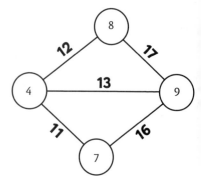

Doubly Delicious

15 two-flavor combinations.
Chocolate with each of the other flavors—CV, CS, CO, CP CB
Vanilla with each of the remaining flavors—VS, VO, VP, VB
Strawberry with each of the remaining flavors—SO, SP, SB
Orange with each of the remaining flavors—OP, OB
Peach with the remaining flavor—PB

Empty Shapes

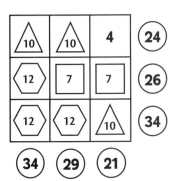

 = 7

= 10

= 12

Figure Out the Figure

Figure 17. Figure 1 has 2 × 4, or 8 dots. Figure 2 has 2 × 5, or 10 dots. Figure 3 has 2 × 6, or 12 dots. Figure 4 has 2 × 7, or 14 dots. So, Figure F has 2 × (F + 3), or 40 dots. 40 ÷ 2 = 20 and 20 − 3 = 17.

Folding Folly
3.

The Frosting on the Cake
4. The picture shows the top of the cake looking down at it.
X = piece with 1 frosted side.
O = piece with 2 frosted sides.
C = piece with 3 frosted sides.

C	O	O	O	O	C
O	X	X	X	X	O
O	X	X	X	X	O
C	O	O	O	O	C

Answers ☀☀☀☀☀☀☀☀☀☀☀☀☀

Full House

a. Lisa, b. Ben, c. Kristen, d. Mike.

⊙ Kristen has 3 times as many people as pets. The only bar that shows a multiple of 3 is Bar c. So, Kristen's house has 6 people and 2 pets.

⊙ Since Ben's house has an odd number of pets and of people, then Bar b must represent Ben's house with 5 people.

⊙ In Lisa's house, there are more pets than people, so there cannot be 8 people and 1 pet. Bar a represents Lisa's house with 4 people, so there must be 5 pets.

⊙ Mike's house must be represented by Bar d—the only bar left.

Get a Homer!

4 bases, 90 feet, 60 feet, 6 inches, 360 feet.

Grid of Squares

4	1	5	(10)
2	7	3	(12)
6	9	8	(23)
(12)	(17)	(16)	

How Many Heads?

48. Here are all the wig (W), nose (N), mouth (M), and eye (E) combinations using Wig #1 (W1):

W1N1M1E1	W1N2M1E1
W1N1M1E2	W1N2M1E2
W1N1M2E1	W1N2M2E1
W1N1M2E2	W1N2M2E2
W1N1M3E1	W1N2M3E1
W1N1M3E2	W1N2M3E2

Here are all the wig (W), nose (N), mouth (M), and eye (E) combinations using Wig #2 (W2):

W2N1M1E1	W2N2M1E1
W2N1M1E2	W2N2M1E2
W2N1M2E1	W2N2M2E1
W2N1M2E2	W2N2M2E2
W2N1M3E1	W2N2M3E1
W2N1M3E2	W2N2M3E2

Here are all the wig (W), nose (N), mouth (M), and eye (E) combinations using Wig #3 (W3):

W3N1M1E1	W3N2M1E1
W3N1M1E2	W3N2M1E2
W3N1M2E1	W3N2M2E1
W3N1M2E2	W3N2M2E2
W3N1M3E1	W3N2M3E1
W3N1M3E2	W3N2M3E2

Here are all the wig (W), nose (N), mouth (M), and eye (E) combinations using Wig #4 (W4):

W4N1M1E1	W4N2M1E1
W4N1M1E2	W4N2M1E2
W4N1M2E1	W4N2M2E1
W4N1M2E2	W4N2M2E2
W4N1M3E1	W4N2M3E1
W4N1M3E2	W4N2M3E2

In the Middle

Page 201. Two hundred pages come before page 201 and two hundred pages come after it.

Just a Matter of Time

Kids and Bikes

Family A, the Valdez family. The graph shows that A has the fewest kids. From the first clue, A and B have to be the Valdez and Chin families. From the second clue, D has to be the Rondo family. That leaves C as the Clark family. From the third clue, C has 2 more kids than the Valdez family. So A has to be the Valdez family.

License Plate Quiz

2	1	3	8	0	5
a	b	c	d	e	f

Since $d + e = d$, then e must be 0.
Since $c \times b = c$, then b must be 1.
Since c is an odd number < 5, then c must be 3.
Since f is an odd number < 7, then f must be 5.
$c - a = b$, so $3 - a = 1$ and $a = 2$.
$d - f = c$, so $d - 5 = 3$ and $d = 8$.

Marble Garble

12—8 red and 4 yellow.

Red	Yellow	Total Marbles
2	1	3 (*not* a multiple of 4)
4	2	6 (*not* a multiple of 4)
6	3	9 (*not* a multiple of 4)
8	**4**	**12 (a multiple of 4)**

MATTHEW'S PATTERN

40. Matthew's name has 7 letters, 2 of which are T's. Divide 140 letters by the 7 letters in his name—$140 \div 7 = 20$. Writing his name 20 times means that there will be 20 x 2, or 40 T's.

A "Month" of Sundays

Monday. Christy knows that there are 30 days in September. She is walking to school on September 2. This is a Monday. The day before, September 1, must have been a Sunday in order for there to be four more Sundays in the month. The next four Sundays are September 8, 15, 22, and 29. So Christy's September 30th birthday will be on a Monday.

Answers ☀ ☀ ☀ ☀ ☀ ☀ ☀ ☀ ☀ ☀ ☀ ☀

Moving Money

There is a total of $1.20 so, in order to have equal amounts, each kid must end up with 40¢.

Tyler gives Chris 1 dime.
Chris gives Justine 1 nickel.
Justine gives Tyler 1 quarter.

After exchanging coins, each of the kids has 40¢—Tyler with 1 quarter, 1 dime, 1 nickel; Chris with 4 dimes; and Justine with 3 dimes, 2 nickels.

A Mystery
2378

Nine Is Fine

1 (x) 3 (+) 8 (−) 4 (+) 2 = 9

Now You See Them...Now You Don't

17 is the least; 23 is the greatest.

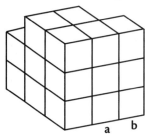

There could be three 2-cube stacks hidden, one stack behind "a" and two behind "b."

Number Cube

24. The six faces of the cube are 19, 20, 21, 22, 23, and 24.

Number Puzzle

30. ☐ and △ could be 7 and 8 or 6 and 9. Either way their sum is 15. 2 x 15 = 30

On the Way to 200

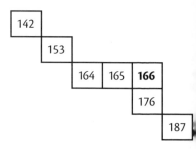

One Brick at a Time

3 colors

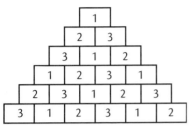

Pizza with the Works

6 pieces of pepperoni,
12 mushrooms, 9 olives.
Make a table to show possible combinations.

P	M	O	Total Pieces
2	4	1	7
3	6	3	12
4	8	5	17
5	10	7	22
6	12	9	27

Pounds-a-Plenty

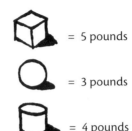

= 5 pounds

= 3 pounds

= 4 pounds

Both the cylinder and cube on scale A are also on scale B. So subtract their total weight, 9 pounds, from scale B to get the weight of the sphere—3 pounds. Now you know that each of the spheres on scale C weighs 3 pounds. Subtract the total weight of the spheres, 6 pounds, from 16 pounds. That means that the two cubes on scale C weigh a total of 10 pounds, or 5 pounds each. Now you know that the cube on scale A weighs 5 pounds. That means that the cylinder weighs 4 pounds.

Real or Fake?

He can put the 3-gram, 5-gram, and 8-gram weights, a total of 16 grams, on the other side of the balance. At the same time, he can put the 1-gram weight on the side with the necklace. If the scale is in balance this way, he will know that the necklace weighs 15 grams.

Answers

Ripped Receipt

Cereal $3.79, Chicken $3.05, Orange Juice $2.79, Total $15.84.

Roll 'Em

The probability of rolling two numbers whose product is an even multiple of 3 is $\frac{15}{36}$, or $\frac{5}{12}$.
The even multiples of 3 are 6, 12 18, 24, 30, 36. There are 36 possible products for a roll of two number cubes. 15 of these are even multiples of 3.

Same Sums

11. Every pair of numbers on opposite faces add up to 19.
The number 8 is on the top of the cube, so 11 must be on the bottom because 8 + 11 = 19.

SASHA'S PATTERN

S. Sasha's name has 5 letters.
If she writes it 18 times she will have written 90 letters because 5 × 18 = 90. As she writes the "S" to begin her name again she will be writing the 91st letter.

Shape Totals

$\triangle_7$ + $\bigcirc_6$ + $\bigcirc_6$ = 19

$\triangle_7$ + $\boxed{8}$ = 15

$\triangle_7$ + $\bigcirc_6$ = 13

$\square$ = $\underline{8}$

$\triangle$ = $\underline{7}$

$\bigcirc$ = $\underline{6}$

Six Slices or Eight?

Whether the whole pizza is cut into 6 pieces or 8 pieces, if Wanda eats them all, she will be eating a whole pizza! $\frac{6}{6} = 1$ and $\frac{8}{8} = 1$

Some Sums

17	80
32	27
21	45
53	52

(97) (59) (66) (105)

(123) (204)

Stamp It!

Two 33¢ stamps, one 32¢ stamp, two 24¢ stamps.

Think "Snow"!

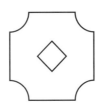

Three Shapes

$\boxed{9}$ + $\boxed{9}$ + 6 = 24

$\boxed{9}$ + (2) + ⟨3⟩ = 14

⟨3⟩ + ⟨3⟩ + ⟨3⟩ + 10 = 19

$\square$ = 9

$\bigcirc$ = 2

⬡ = 3

Answers

Try for "A" 13!

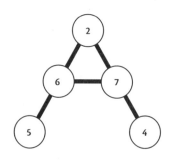

or

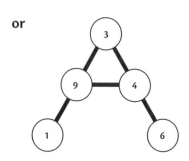

A Walking Problem
0 blocks.
0 + 3 + 6 + 9 + 12 = 30

Watch the Hands
10 times. The hands pass each other once each hour except during the 11:00 hour.

Where is 79?
Row 16. Divide. 79 ÷ 5 = 15 R4 means that there are 15 rows of 5. Number 79 is the fourth number in Row 16.

Who Likes Basketball?
Andrew. Dan goes to the pool, so he likes swimming. Kenesha is a goalie, so she likes soccer. That leaves Andrew and Betty. Since Andrew is the same age as his twin, Kenesha, he cannot be the oldest. So Betty must be the oldest. She likes baseball. Andrew is left as the one who likes basketball.

Words Worth
zoo (26 + 15 + 15 = 56)
bear (2 + 5 + 1 + 18 = 26)

Yikes!
2 ants and 6 spiders.